$\mathcal{S}$ILENCING ME

OVERCOMING OBSTACLES TO SPIRITUAL DISCERNMENT

SAMONTIA WHYTE MILLER

ISBN: 978-1-965635-90-2 (paperback)

Printed in the United States of America

ENDORSEMENTS

This book, Silencing Me: Overcoming Obstacles to Spiritual Discernment, challenges us to come to Abba, naked and unashamed. No masks. The real us. That we may be healed and receive freedom, grace, and peace to be who He has called us to be without fear or judgment.

Samontia boldly shares her journey to overcoming her own obstacles in gaining spiritual discernment, likening the process to a garden. Hard truths are shared as she reveals that what we might think is the worst thing that could happen to us could be our "garden": "that dirt is not the end, it is where new life begins." No "mess" is a waste; there is purpose to be found in it.

Several tips, tools, and strategies are shared throughout to help navigate life's distractions, hear God's still voice amidst the chaos that often grips our minds, and focus our gaze on Him.

We are encouraged to meditate, journal, fast, and pray, amongst other beneficial spiritual practices, to keep our hearts and minds steadfast on things above.

Having read this book, you will come out on the other side, renewed, encouraged, and driven to spend more time in God's presence.

The privilege is mine to endorse this book.

Tiffany Wright

Author and Minister of Religion
Church of God of Prophecy

As a therapist, I deeply value resources that meet people exactly where they are, and *Silencing Me: Overcoming Obstacles to Spiritual Discernment* does just that. A deeply relatable guide for wherever you find yourself on your spiritual journey, this book meets readers at the honest, often messy, intersection of everyday life and faith. Through the ordinary moments of her own story, the author weaves lived experiences with thoughtful insight, offering lessons that resonate deeply with the heart.

Readers can expect unfiltered honesty, vulnerability, and approachability throughout, alongside powerful themes of growth and resilience. With courage and grace, Samontia shares her personal testimony, revealing what it looks like to continue trusting God's presence, even in life's most painful seasons.

I recommend this book, not only as a dear friend and fellow believer but also as a therapist, as the author creates a safe and inviting space for readers to explore faith amid life's complexities. In a therapeutic relationship, healing begins with mutual respect, clear communication, and a shared commitment to growth. In the same way, this book acts as a guide embodying unconditional positive regard—offering grace, compassion, and understanding to the reader in a profoundly Christ-like manner.

The book is a gift for anyone, whether spiritually grounded or newly embarking on a journey to hear God's voice above all the noises of the world and those within. Whatever season of life has led you here, may these pages refresh your spirit, restore your hope, and encourage you to stay the course and dwell in abundance.

Tiffany Scafe Norman MSW, LSW, LCAC-A.

Mental Health Therapist

To those who were silenced by fear, shame or anxiety;
May you discover that God's voice has always been louder
than what tried to quiet you.

SILENCING ME

TABLE OF CONTENTS

Endorsements...iii

Foreword... 13

Preface: The Face I Wore 17

Introduction: Sowing for the Future... 21

Chapter 1: Crown of Thorns: Resilience Amid Adversity 29

Chapter 2: Tilling the Soil: Embracing Change and Letting Go 41

Chapter 3: Seeds and Roots: Uprooting and Planting 51

Chapter 4: Pruning: Letting Go Of What No Longer Serves You 67

Chapter 5: Nurturing Growth: Cultivating Patience and Persistence 77

Chapter 6: Budding Possibilities: Living a Life of Purpose and Meaning 87

Chapter 7: Harvesting the Fruits of Spiritual Discernment 101

Reflection: Evolution: Stillness. Discernment. Spiritual Growth. 113

Acknowledgments 121

About the Author 123

FOREWORD

It is both an honor and a privilege to write the foreword to *Silencing Me: Overcoming Obstacles to Spiritual Discernment* by Samontia Whyte Miller.

I have had the privilege of knowing Samontia for the past three years, and during that time, she has consistently stood out as someone with a genuine willingness to serve, listen, and take initiative, reflecting a maturity that comes from a deep desire to honor God and love His people well.

Over my years of pastoral ministry, I have learned that one of the greatest battles believers face is not a lack of faith, but a loss of clarity; an inability to hear God's voice clearly amid the noise of life, trauma, expectation, and survival. Many learn how to endure, how to press forward, how to serve well, yet quietly struggle to recognize themselves beneath the layers they've built, just to make it through.

This book speaks directly to that sacred tension. After attending a "Women By Design" conference, hosted by our church, Samontia shared with me a reflection, and her words revealed not only honesty, but spiritual sensitivity – a heart that had taken the time to sit with God, to reflect, and to respond with obedience. That moment affirmed what I believe this book will do for many: give language to silent struggles and permission to return to who God originally called us to be.

Silencing Me is not a quick fix, nor is it a surface-level devotional. It is an invitation to slow down, to uproot what no longer serves us, to tend to the soil of our hearts, and to relearn how to listen.

Through rich metaphor, biblical truth, and personal testimony, Samontia guides readers through the process of spiritual discernment with grace, patience, and compassion. Her writing reflects the same servant-hearted posture she lives out daily – gentle, intentional, and deeply rooted in faith.

What makes this work especially powerful is its sincerity. This book does not shy away from pain, nor does it glorify it. Instead, it honors the God who redeems every season, who prunes in love, and who paints masterpieces from broken pieces. It speaks to the weary believer, the faithful servant, the woman who has survived but longs to truly live, and assures them that God has never lost sight of who they are.

As you turn these pages, I encourage you to read with an open heart and a willing spirit. Allow yourself to pause, reflect, pray, and listen. This journey is not about becoming someone new, but about returning—rooted, restored, and renewed to the truth of who you are in God. May this book meet you exactly where you are, and may it gently lead you into the clarity, peace, and discernment that come from being fully known, fully seen, and fully loved by Him.

With love and expectation,

Pastor Jillian Thomas

Emmanuel Apostolic Church

THE FACE I WORE

I have worn a face for years that I no longer recognise. Truth is, I don't even know if God recognises me.

The mask was shaped by survival and fear, even calling me timid when I once was bold.

I learned to speak in voices that weren't mine, to smile when my spirit was weary, to blend in when my heart longed to break free.

Now the mask feels heavy. But wearing it was easy. I tried to understand my calling and to create the persona that would wear it well, but today I recognised that the mantle I have been called to carry requires me only to be myself.

So now the mask cracks in my hands as I look for what's real beneath it. And in the quiet, I wonder: *Does God still know me under all these layers?*

But maybe the truth is this: *God has never lost sight of me. Even when I lost sight of myself, even when I hid behind the faces I made, His knowing never faltered. His love never mistook the mask for the woman.*

GOD IS THE MASTER PAINTER

My life, once a blank canvas, now scarred and messy, only telling the tale of how He has been writing my story.

All I can think of is God holding me in His arms, knowing that every brushstroke is Grace with Mercy and Truth, giving me a testimony.

He's painting me into the masterpiece I was meant to become.

So now, step by step, I walk the road back. Not to who I was, but to who I truly am, opening myself up to the strokes of the Master Artist.

Each tear, each prayer, each moment of honesty is a stone laid on the path of restoration. And maybe this is what grace looks like—not the sudden fixing of what is broken, but the gentle uncovering, the revealing of what is still alive beneath the ashes, allowing the Painter's hand to work slowly, patiently, beautifully.

In that truth, I find rest: *I am known. I am seen. I am loved. And I am under the hand of Jesus Christ, the Master Artist, who paints with purpose—turning life into art, shadow into light, masks into true faces.*

SOWING FOR THE FUTURE

The question of how to hear God's voice amid a chaotic world resonates deeply in today's society. Many of us are victims of social expectations, owing to the constant influx of information, the pressure to perform, the idea to fit in, and the internal chatter of our own minds. Thinking about this question feels particularly acute, and since all these factors often mute the still, small voice that offers guidance and peace in our day-to-day lives, we must develop strategies to help us manage the noise and listen to God's voice. To demonstrate the idea of overcoming obstacles to spiritual discernment, I think of changes like shedding old leaves, leading to the growth of new leaves and renewal, likening it to a garden.

The garden is made up of many plants and must be watered in order to thrive, just as our souls need to be watered by God in order to grow. I use the analogy of a garden because it goes through many seasons of growth and transition, and if you do not nurture it, the trees perish. In the same way, there are seasons in which you will have to shed your own ideas to embrace new ways of thinking, and there are seasons in which you will have to depend on the gardener who is God—your source—to take you through your autumn when growth can feel long, often taking more time than you expect.

Have you ever felt like everything is taking too long?

When this thought comes to mind, you may say to yourself, "I am older now, but I still don't know my purpose." You may begin to feel frustrated because things are neither happening in the sequence you were hoping for nor at the pace you were hoping for. In these moments where you wrestle with your thoughts, remember that God's purpose in your life cannot be rushed. Truth is, the time at which you feel buried, God is doing His best work because you are being watered to grow into your true potential. When you begin to hide in the shadow of the Almighty, He protects you from all that is brewing at the surface, while He works on your heart and gives you the wisdom and strength to fight and rise above all the odds that you face.

When God renews your heart and mind beneath the surface, He will grant you the power to conquer all things at the surface level. The 'water' that has been welling up in your heart from all the hurt you feel will rise from beneath the ground and saturate the surface. What is meant to be fruitful will be watered, and what is meant to harm you will be destroyed, as reflected in the scripture **"And it shall come**

to pass, that like as I have watched over them, to pluck up, and to break down, and to throw down, and to destroy, and to afflict; so will I watch over them, to build, and to plant, saith the Lord." (Jeremiah 31:28 - KJV), and further evidenced in Matthew 15:13 and 1 Corinthians 3:6.

I wonder what the first thought is when someone plants a tree. To me, a seed in the ground seems fragile, in that it can be easily lost if the territory in which it is planted is not marked. It may be washed away by a storm or may even wither away due to drought. In the beginning, there is nothing visible above the soil, but with the right environment, sunlight and water reach that seed, and in time you will begin to see a tiny seedling reaching up through the soil, and in the long term a strong tree. The phenomenon itself is supernatural, demonstrating that while we have some control over the process, there is a reliance on the Creator to give life to what we have planted. Consider whether we build our lives in a similar way, planting a fragile seed, hoping for structure and strength, yet without deeply anchoring in God. What happens when we experience drought, winds, or rain?

It begs the question, *What foundation are we building our lives on?*

Matthew 7:24-27 teaches us of the wise and foolish men, citing those who hear and act on His words as wise and those who hear and do not act as foolish men. This parable is further illustrated by the wise men building on the rock and the foolish men building on the sand, encouraging us to build a foundation that lasts. You may ask yourself: *What foundation am I trusting to keep me grounded when the storms come? What roots are in place to hold me steady when the wind blows? Will my current structure stand firm if one area of my life is tested? What are some roots of entanglement that I need to cut off? Am I using the power which Christ placed in me to uproot every "giant" threatening my foundation?*

At the juncture where I was positioned to ask myself these questions, it felt like I was challenging the belief systems I had put in place to help me navigate life. Not only did the answers to these questions provide clarity, but they also forced me to start over in more ways than one. Notwithstanding this, the fear of starting over often weighed heavily on me, leading me to decide that, whatever the situation, I would make it work. Some may consider it a good quality, and sometimes I believe it is one of my greatest strengths. However, a perspective like this can be quite crippling when God is calling us to change and embrace a new beginning, by shedding and putting aside what we know, and trusting Him to take us into the unknown. To move from this point to allowing God to direct my path, I had to accept that starting over is not a sign of failure. Instead, it is walking in a new direction, with more insights into what did not work and the knowledge of what needs to be done to obtain a more favourable outcome. In that moment, my strength came not only from rejecting judgment from others but also from rejecting self-judgment, and looking to my ultimate Gardner, the Author and Finisher of my faith, to order my steps.

Once I was able to silence the voices long enough to hear God's promise, I began to accept that reseeding is a process that I must go through. First, the seed must be planted and given the right environment to thrive. This includes: watering, fertilising, and allowing sunlight for seed germination. Nurturing my soul through His Word helped me to adapt to new ways of thinking and being. This equipped me with the strength, coverage, and perseverance to make it through the autumn season, and the understanding that when the season of dull beauty came to an end, I had made it to spring, ready to thrive and bear fruit. In that moment, I was comforted, knowing that the fruitful areas of my life would thrive, while the unfruitful areas would be pruned, as seen in John 15:1-2, which states **"I am the true vine, and my Father is the gardener. He cuts off every branch in me that bears no fruit, while every branch that does bear fruit he prunes so that it will be even more fruitful." (NIV).**

The definition of your new beginning is not just about starting over but about building the right foundation, understanding growth in a whole new way, and embracing change. You can begin to build your life in a new way—like a tree planted by streams of water, its roots deep, its trunk firm, and its leaves green—instead of building your life like a domino tower, which is fragile and ready to fall with one poke. Though the "domino effect" often evokes collapse, it also reminds us that one small, consistent action can make room for a big impact, demonstrating how our faith creates avenues for growth. When we trust, we grow. When we grow, we bear fruit. When we bear fruit, others are stirred. When we seek God in the midst of our sickness and are healed, we see God's power and are then able to speak healing into others.

Our faith brings healing; healing brings hope; hope builds a character that trusts in Him. As you start your new beginning, God is calling you to silence the external and internal noises that negatively impact you hearing His voice, and this book is designed to help you do just that. It provides guidance to foster deeper spiritual listening, offering practical strategies and exercises to help you make space to hear from Him. With a focus on journaling, mindfulness, meditation, and prayer as essential tools, we will examine methods for reducing both internal and external noise, and explore how doubt, fear, anxiety, shame, and constant distractions affect our listening and prevent us from hearing God's direction. In assessing these obstacles, you will see empathy and doable solutions, with a non-judgmental approach to self-introspection and problem-solving. On this journey, you will learn that listening to God is a process of self-discovery through a gradual unveiling of a deeper relationship with yourself and God. As you delve into the pages of this book, you will engage in silent reflection and active participation, both expected to reveal God's presence as you move through your healing process.

Let's take this journey together, a step toward creating your own new beginning.

Let's uproot.
Let's plant.
Let's become rooted.
Let's grow.

And let our lives become trees that are strong enough to withstand storms, and fruitful enough to sow hope into others. Embrace the journey and allow yourself to be guided by the wisdom waiting to be discovered within.

POWER OF DIVINE CONSCIOUSNESS

"And be not conformed to this world: but be ye transformed by the renewing of your mind, that ye may prove what is that good, and acceptable, and perfect, will of God."

—Romans 12:2 KJV

CHAPTER 1

CROWN OF THORNS: RESILIENCE AMID ADVERSITY

We live in an age that does not sleep, pause, or permit stillness. Everything shouts. Everything demands. Often, this leads to sensory overload. Instead of enhancing our lives, constant stimulation often leaves us feeling overburdened, exhausted, and disengaged, making it harder for us to develop a deeper relationship with God. What becomes more deafening are the relentless streams of information from the media and our internal thoughts that fuel self-doubt; both often speak louder than the scriptures and positive thoughts we need to thrive in today's world. Externally, modern life pulls us in every possible direction, while internally we become prisoners of our own thoughts, trapped in a cycle of worry and self-criticism. This pervasive noise not only undermines the basis of silent reflection but can also erode its foundation, which is important for spiritual growth.

Consider, for instance, the average individual's day. When the alarm clock goes off, what do you do first? I think about getting out of bed to beat the traffic. But, before that, there comes the instantaneous urge to check my phone's notifications, even before giving thanks for being alive. At this moment, I wonder: did I get a personal email I need to attend to now, or shall I simply do a quick scroll to see what is happening on social media? Of course, the road is a blare of car horns, and do not get me started on those early bloomers who blast their music early in the morning. On the way to work, I use navigation apps to take the detours necessary to avoid traffic. What is most important here is the fact that I listen to the soft and gentle voice that is leading and guiding me to get me to work in the shortest possible time, but what is most significant is that I often keep the windows up in order to manage the external noise so I can stay on track and focus on my destination.

I finally get to work; an actual work day, filled with deadlines, meetings, and disruptions. When I get home, I often want to make a cup of tea and greet my coworkers before I begin a task. In all of this, a few questions generally plague my mind. *Where is the time for the gym? Where is the time to parent? Where is the time to be a wife? Where is the time to take care of myself? Where is the space in this hectic world for introspection, prayer and general spiritual connection?* The foregoing illustration has a profound effect on spiritual practices. Because our days are filled with what we equate to life's necessities, we may find it increasingly difficult to pray or meditate, as we are unable to stop the constant barrage of noises from within us and around us.

I identify the challenges that we face in making space for spiritual growth as a divine struggle. What has become even more daunting is that a lack of spiritual connection with God exacerbates alienation, leading to feelings of emptiness, spiritual dryness, and a waning of faith, leaving believers struggling to find a sense of peace, purpose, and connection with God. To address these issues, we need to become resilient people who make space for God and our relationship with Him, even when we are bombarded by other areas of our lives.

It is often said the strongest flowers bloom in the harshest soil, just as the mightiest soldiers emerge from the toughest battles. Notwithstanding this, resilience is not merely about surviving, but it is about thriving in the face of insurmountable obstacles. It is a dual force: one that embodies the strength to endure adversity and, more profoundly, a mirror that reflects the depth and quality of our faith in the Lord, as revealed through His biblical principles.

When I ponder what it means to stand firm when everything around me is shaking, I am drawn to one of nature's less attractive but deeply instructive teachers: The Crown of Thorns. The name of the plant connotes both beauty and endurance—beauty in the pain. In my own journey, the face I wore was my physical defence. Laced with thorns, it was a sign of survival, my coping mechanism, and my way of

31

ensuring I could not get hurt first; an irony I was too hurt to identify at the time. This defence mechanism only padded me with years of fear, grief, stress, and anxiety. While these trauma responses are all normal, I recognised that God's desire for me was not to sit in that amount of hurt, and here I am writing this book, seeing the mask fall to the ground, feeling naked and fearful like the little girl I once was.

Every step I took to get me to where I am, though successful, only placed layer upon layer of masks on the woman I was always meant to become. The myth of "I am the strong one" is what I wrestled with for years. At one point, it felt like it was too much to surrender to the me I created. So, I walked around sometimes with a heavy heart, wondering when I would feel the me I once knew, and finally, the day came when everything was expected to change. There I was with my own thoughts and feelings, realising I did nothing but pad on the many faces that kept me sane. At this juncture, I was faced with becoming resilient, not being unaffected but recovering, adjusting, and moving forward as the new me, and leaving behind the persona I created in my coping season. Once I totally surrendered to God, my faith began to act as a protective thorn, not keeping me isolated but keeping me standing firm with my beliefs in Christ. Having gone through this process, I realized that I would bloom through hardships, not just when they have come to an end.

While writing this section, I paused to offer a prayer of thanksgiving, as this reflection reminded me of how much I have fought to silence myself and the world around me, so that I might hear God speak to me and speak through me. God is calling you to do the same. The anxiety felt on a daily basis is not by chance. It is literally the devil's way of keeping you bound and preventing you from releasing what God has placed inside you.

Since entering the working world, I have been more anxious than I ever imagined. I know my worth; I am great at what I do, but I am still unusually anxious sometimes. If you ask me why, I would say I do not have any reason to be anxious. There are some tasks I can do in my sleep, but I am still anxious about them. Anxiety is the thief of joy and peace that the Lord has promised us. It exists to rob us of our desire to lean on and trust the promises of God. Many of us spend a significant portion of our lives trying not to worry, yet worrying anyway. We ask God to give us the strength to overcome our fears, and then we worry whether He will. Although we are confident that He exists and will fulfill our needs according to His riches in glory, we worry about whether He will or whether we are good enough to receive it. This occurs because we cling to only a portion of the truth, keeping us trapped in a state of anxiety where it can be tempting to think that failure, uncertainty, and concern are the only aspects of life. Because I developed an understanding of how anxiety affects my faith, I was able to identify how the seed was planted in my heart and began reinforcing the truth of God's Word in my life to subdue anxiety.

What are some of the things you have always been anxious about?

After you are able to answer this question, think about how the anxiety cripples your spiritual listening ears, and what strategies you will employ to become resilient listeners, even when you face challenges.

A strategy you can employ to silence anxiety is prayer. When you pray, ask God to speak to you, sit in silence, and wait for Him to speak. I guarantee you that He will provide a word of comfort to take you through whichever season you are navigating. After this first encounter, be intentional and be consistent, and your ears will mature and become inclined to His voice over time. To cultivate a new mindset, you must totally surrender your desires to Him and trust His promises to make your life new, knowing that His plans are better than your plans anyway.

Being able to subject your anxiety to the blood of Jesus means you will experience His peace, joy, hope, and love. You are reminded of His Word, **"Do not be anxious about anything, but in every situation, by prayer and petition, with thanksgiving, present your requests to God. And the peace of God, which transcends all understanding, will guard your hearts and your minds in Christ Jesus." (see Philippians 4:6-7 - NIV).**

Building resilience requires a growth mindset. It requires persistence and grit, along with adaptability, flexibility, optimism, and hope. It is our commitment to continue moving toward our goals despite obstacles, delays, or temporary unsuccess. The adversities we face lead to redemption if we manage our true feelings about them in a healthy way. Some strategies that are useful for navigating the challenges you face in day-to-day life include journaling, therapy, praying, and submitting to God. Without resilience, potential often stays unrealized, because the path to blooming is rarely straight or easy.

The first step in becoming resilient is to acknowledge the problem. We must recognize just how overwhelming the pace and pressure of modern life can be and how deeply they impact our spiritual well-being, and that the noises we encounter are not only external but also internal, including distractions, doubts, anxieties, and constant mental chatter.

After acknowledging the issues, we must understand that cultivating a life of spiritual depth requires more than good intentions; it demands deliberate choices. This means we must carve out time for reflection to develop tools for managing external and internal noise. For instance, when you reflect on a day, you can identify your own shortcomings and address them by creating a to-do list for the next day, deliberately structuring your day to make room for God, and setting aside time for rest so you are equipped to take on the next day. It takes discipline, focused effort, and a willingness to prioritize our spiritual growth above the endless demands that clamor for our attention each day.

We must then learn to still the racing thoughts, quiet the constant inner dialogue, and release the anxieties that so often drown out the voice of God. Practices like mindfulness, contemplative prayer, and meditation become essential on this journey, as they open the door to inner stillness and help create the sacred space where true spiritual listening can begin. This journey in itself is a spiritual practice that results in gradual transformation. It is not a quick fix, but rather it teaches patience and perseverance, which often lead to finding peace, purpose, and connecting with God.

The second step is understanding that in the middle of all the noise, God speaks, but not as we might expect. God, instead, chooses stillness. A whisper. A breath. A voice so soft it can be missed in the rush. The scripture tells us this plainly, as demonstrated when Elijah, the prophet, worn thin by conflict and fear, stood on the mountain waiting for God. In the scriptures, he heard the wind rent the mountains, the earthquake shake the earth, and saw the fire rage, but the voice of God was not present in any of those elements. The passage further illustrates that a gentle whisper came, and Elijah knew that God was speaking (see 1 Kings 19:11-12). This is the paradox we must learn to live with: that the infinite, all-powerful God often speaks with a voice so quiet, it can be heard only by those willing to stop, to hush their souls, and to lean in close to hear what He is saying. It begs the question: *how often do we miss His voice because we are only attuned to the loudest roar?* Think about communication in an intimate relationship or communication in a relationship where one is in power and the other is a subordinate. Would you prefer a roar or a whisper? There is something deeply intimate about a whisper, as it requires closeness, and it does not compete with the world's volume. This is why a spiritual practice, like prayer, is still a lifeline in Christianity today. When you intentionally create space to hear God's voice and become consistent with listening for His instructions, you will become attuned to what He sounds like, as seen in John 10:27: **"My sheep hear my voice, and I know them, and they follow me." (KJV).**

Another aspect of this step is learning to listen for God's voice in unexpected places, not just while you are praying or waiting to hear from Him through a dream, but understanding that He speaks to us in thoughts, words, and deeds in simple day-to-day scenarios like washing dishes or driving to work. This may require you to find a new rhythm, and just saying the simple words *"speak Lord, thy servant heareth" (see 1 Samuel 3:9-10).* In doing so, you will begin to commune with the Lord more often.

Turning down the volume of the world, in truth, is something you may not always be able to do. Instead, God is calling you to discover a rhythm, not by following the patterns of the world, but by intentionally stepping away from them. You can tune your heart to a different frequency to discover the holy invitation hidden beneath the roar: being still and listening intently. Spiritual listening requires resisting the pressure to conform to a culture driven by constant productivity, comparison, and noise, and aligning your life with a different rhythm shaped by grace, rest, and attentiveness to the Spirit. This countercultural posture creates space for a deeper awareness of God's presence and invites you to live not at the world's pace, but at the pace of peace. The scripture reminds us **"And be not conformed to this world: but be ye transformed by the renewing of your mind, that ye may prove what is that good, and acceptable, and perfect, will of God." (see Romans 12:2 - KJV).** Renewed thinking changes our mindset and, through prayer and fasting, allows us to walk in God's likeness and image.

You have learned how to become resilient despite the challenges that hinder you from listening to God's voice. In the chapters to follow, we will explore meaningful ways to quiet the noise—both around us and within us—and to deepen our connection with God. Together, we will explore tested practices such as mindfulness, meditation, and prayer, offering practical guidance to help you listen more closely to the voice of the Spirit. We will also confront the common challenges that hinder spiritual listening by assessing how you can recognise these obstacles and overcome them. Through each step, the goal remains the same: to cultivate a stillness that invites the presence of God and a discernment that leads us into His will through personal reflections, spiritual practices, and support from faith-based communities. The journey begins by recognizing the noise that surrounds and fills us, and by making a conscious commitment to create the inner stillness where God's voice can be truly heard.

BALANCE. TRUST. ALIGNMENT.

"a time to cast away stones, and a time to gather stones together; a time to embrace, and a time to refrain from embracing;"

—Ecclesiastes 3:5 KJV

CHAPTER 2

TILLING THE SOIL: EMBRACING CHANGE AND LETTING GO

Have you ever wondered why in our deepest search for clarity, God's voice seems hardest to find?

This question is a challenge many believers face. In the moments we crave divine direction the most—when we are desperate, uncertain, or burdened with a decision—God often seems quiet, distant, or hidden. But perhaps the issue is not God's silence, but the noise within us. Many times, we have emotional ties with our feelings, sometimes wanting to develop new responses to life's challenges, but often rest on the crutches of what we already know. Doubt, fear, impatience, and pride can cloud our inner landscape, making it difficult to discern the still voice of the Spirit.

Doubt, which frequently appears as a significant barrier to our spiritual development, can take many forms, including questioning the direction in which we believe God is leading us. Even though they are disconcerting, these concerns are a normal part of the journey, and I would consider it a sign of growing faith rather than evidence of a failing one. Simply put, when we question these things, we are able to try the spirit and know the spirit by further identifying evidence of God's existence, love, and faithfulness toward us by evaluating spiritual teachings and experiences that will, in turn, help us to know the spirit of truth (see 1 John 4:1-6).

On the one hand, we have doubt; on the other, fear. One of the challenges we face in this regard is that doubt weakens faith. Because faith is trusting, believing, and leaning on His promises, when doubt is introduced, fear then becomes a natural response. Furthermore, when we begin to doubt what God has said, we create space for fear to grow. Doubt lets us ask the question: *Is this truly God's instruction?* While fear tells us that we need to figure things out on our own.

In the Garden of Eden, Eve's entertaining of the serpent's deceptive questions led her to doubt the Word of God. This triggered a response of fear, leading to her disobedience, and her and Adam's consumption of the forbidden fruit (see Genesis 3:1-10). Eve clearly felt that God had left her and was not with her after the fruit was eaten. Though she must have felt this way, we know God was still with her, but here, abandonment was introduced, highlighted by her retreating as she hid. This story, along with the story of Peter walking on water in Matthew 14:28-31, highlights how doubt causes us to lose focus on the bigger picture and can, in essence, change the path we are meant to take. This illustration shows how doubt becomes the spiritual opening for fear to take root in our lives.

Another obstacle to spiritual discernment is impatience. Spiritual listening requires a posture of waiting on God's timing; not hearing from Him on the things we want to learn about in our time, but trusting that God will provide the answers when He knows it is time for us to listen, learn, and act. Impatience pushes us to determine our plans and map out how to achieve them without hearing from God. A key ideology that causes us to act in this manner is one that positions everything we come into contact with as urgent. Because of this, we replace trust with control—wanting to take action now—thinking we need to ensure that the goals are in place and the strategies are determined; when in truth, we did not wait to determine if the goal was aligned with His purpose of what we are to step into in that given moment.

Impatience can also allow us to feel anxiety and further put us in a position to mistake what we feel or hear within us as that of the Master's voice, and when we act on these, we may confuse activity or movement with progress, all the while being thrust onto a whole different path, which God did not intend for us to go onto. The story that stands out for me in this regard is the children of Israel asking for a King, rejecting Samuel, and ultimately God's rule over Israel (see 1 Samuel 8:5-6). This story teaches us that, as human beings, we are prone to seeking human solutions rather than His unique divine plan, and, importantly, that rejecting God's favour and authority over our lives can have negative consequences. We can even assess Saul's performance of the sacrifice in 1st Samuel 13. Though he was instructed to wait on Samuel, he became impatient and made the sacrifice on his own. In turn, he lost God's favour. While his actions were a result of impatience, they also demonstrated a peevish disposition toward the instruction he received from God and, in essence, showed that he was not receptive to the process God intended for him to follow.

True discernment grows in the soil of patience (see Isaiah 30:18). Having parents who engaged in farming allows me to reflect on what the soil looks like after a harvest. Hear me out, the imagery of the hard soil, old grass, and weeds is sometimes reflective of the state we are in, but worst of all, there has been no harvest, because we bore no fruit. Until you till the soil, nothing new has a chance to grow—the preparation, breaking the old, letting the earth breathe—is powerful imagery of what takes place when God invites us to change by letting go of old habits, old identities, and entrenched hurt. The heart must be cleared of stones and weeds and softened through surrender to prepare the ground for God to work in.

While writing this chapter, I had one of the biggest revelations. I literally do not have a clue what I want to say; I thought I did initially because I followed the correct process by mapping out the issues I wanted to explore and did my research. What became evident is that I know what I wanted to say, but I had not heard from God about exactly what He wants to share with those who will be impacted by this book. So, here I was on a Saturday afternoon; my son was watching a developmental programme on TV with his grandad, and my mom and husband were fast asleep on the floor. The posture of the latter spoke so much volume, and that gave me the revelation I needed to speak about pride in this book. Lying on the floor highlights humility; they were not engaging in this behaviour because they had nowhere to sleep, but because they were humble and felt they were in a safe space, free to fall asleep that way. That's when it dawned on me: spiritual listening requires humility—the openness to be vulnerable, to receive, to be corrected, and to acknowledge that one does not know everything. Pride, on the other hand, often insists that one already knows everything or does not need any form of direction or guidance, and has a significant impact on spiritual discernment, which is the ability to differentiate between what is spiritually unsound and what is spiritually sound. Spiritual discernment requires a surrendered mind and heart posture, which often calls for patience and an openness to being guided and to following unexpected directions. As you lean into this, you can identify and set aside pride that may occur in the following ways:

1. Creating filtration criteria that validate self-interest. This is a form of selective listening that affirms only what one's intention is, while muting anything that challenges it. Instead, you are to create a set of criteria that allows you to lay aside your own

interests and create an atmosphere in which you can hear from God.

2. Mistaking personal expectation for revelation. This is the use of spiritual language to justify personal agendas. This is the classic *"God told me to carry out a particular action,"* if this is a belief that comes only because it aligns with what the individual wants to do. Often, this happens because the word is not surrendered to or tried, and the individual is excited to step into what he has heard in himself. Instead, whenever you believe that you have received a word from God, ensure it aligns with the scriptures rather than personal beliefs.

Embracing change starts with letting go. God calls us to **"Remember ye not the former things, neither consider the things of old [because he is calling us to something great, saying], Behold, I will do a new thing; now it shall spring forth; shall ye not know it? I will even make a way in the wilderness and rivers in the desert." (Isaiah 43:18-19 - KJV).** This charge, as found in the scriptures, tells us that change is a necessary transformation that supports spiritual growth, urging us to let go of old habits and ways of thinking and to embrace the new life offered through faith in God.

Before new growth can happen, the soil must be tilled. In the process of tilling, the soil is broken down and turned over, then exposed to air and light. Going back to my childhood, this process, as I recall, is not tidy; it is messy preparation. Letting go works the same way. It is about gently turning a new leaf, acknowledging that some seasons have run their course, and that making space for new things means stepping away from what is familiar. Tilling the soil does not reject the past; instead, it uses it. All the nutrients from the previous crops become part of the foundation for what will be planted next. In the same way, letting go of doubt, fear, impatience, and pride makes way for the planting of new seeds in your life.

Change is inevitable, and believe me, I understand why you may be afraid. You resist change because of possible uncertainty and fear of what life will look like when you walk a new path. You may even struggle with a loss of control due to your attachment to social norms, or even by trying to be the potter when we are simply the clay. To help you understand this journey, know that letting go is different from giving up. Letting go is intentional and charts the way for growth, whereas giving up is marked by defeat. Knowing that there is a difference between letting go and giving up, are you willing to take the step?

In the process of letting go, there is an active need for forgiveness and closure. We must forgive ourselves for settling into our own thoughts and disobeying God's direction, and find closure in Him directing our paths. This is a daily process that begins with acceptance. To embrace change, you must remove the mask of fear and accept where you are now, knowing that God is working on you to move you into your next season. Once the soil is ready, the future will plant itself. Following acceptance, you can begin to frame what this new dispensation of Grace looks like for you. In doing so, you should begin to see change as an opportunity rather than a threat, recognising that a cognitive shift in perspective can help you ease into the transition. Thereafter, you begin to adapt what God is teaching by following His instructions, one step at a time, revealing your strength and resilience. Then you navigate the new journey, taking one step at a time, showing yourself compassion and treating yourself gently as you learn new things and build your support system.

Here are affirmations to help you in this phase of your journey:

1. I am allowed to outgrow old stories.
2. Lord, I trust You to take me into the unknown. I surrender my heart and mind to You.
3. Change is not a threat. God has called me to change and evolve.
4. I release what does not nourish my spiritual life, and make room for spiritual growth.
5. Through God, I am rooted, resilient, and prepared for what comes next.
6. I will not be conformed to this world, but be transformed by the renewing of my mind (see Romans 12:2 - KJV).
7. "Be strong and of good courage, fear not, nor be afraid of them: for the Lord thy God, he it is that doth

go with thee; he will not fail thee, nor forsake thee."(Deuteronomy 31:6 - KJV).

WHOLE. COMPLETE.

"Not that I speak in respect of want: for I have learned, in whatsoever state I am, therewith to be content."

—Philippians 4:11 KJV

CHAPTER 3

SEEDS AND ROOTS: UPROOTING AND PLANTING

Building a strong Christ-like foundation in our lives often calls for prayer, meditation, fasting, solitude, and service. Beyond these structured principles lies a more subtle, yet equally powerful, divine Guidance: your 'gut feeling', commonly called intuitive knowing, where you can tap into a sudden flash of insight. Make no mistake, your gut feeling is not your own drive nor an interpretation of a stimulus, but represents a deeper connection to the Creator of our being, guiding you into a place where the conscious mind faces the spiritual mind, often revealing a deeper truth beyond the reach of logical reasoning. However, we live in a fast-paced, information-saturated world, where we often drown out this quiet voice with the incessant demands of our external environment and the constant chatter of our inner thoughts.

Developing the ability to recognise and trust God's voice requires conscious effort, practice, and a willingness to step beyond the confines of purely rational thinking. In doing so, we become seeds, allowing for a season of planting and nurturing so we can begin to grow roots and eventually become rooted. Growth starts first with a small seed being planted, buried in darkness, unseen, pressed beneath the weight of the soil, and some plants will only grow strong if they are grounded deep beneath the soil.

There is a strange tension in the process of growth: the conundrum of being planted. Both the planting of a seed and being buried look the same. Both involve being covered by dirt, hidden, and surrounded by darkness. To the untrained eye, both appear to be endings, but through the spiritual lens, the latter may represent the ending of life, while the former is the beginning of life. It is what happens underground that determines the strength of what rises above it, and even if it is dead and decaying, God can still give life, as purported in the scripture: **"And he said unto me, Son of man, can these bones live? And I answered, O Lord GOD, thou knowest. Again he said unto me, Prophesy upon these bones, and say unto them, O ye dry bones, hear the word of the LORD. Thus saith the Lord GOD unto these bones; Behold, I will cause breath to enter into you, and ye shall live: and I will lay sinews upon you, and will bring up flesh upon you, and cover you with skin, and put breath in you, and ye shall live; and ye shall know that I am the LORD."** (Ezekiel 37:3-6 – KJV). As a powerful vision of Israel's hopelessness and God's promise of miraculous spiritual and physical restoration, this scripture is a testament to God's intent for spiritual renewal among believers. Dissecting the idea of being buried alive takes me back to my childhood.

There I was, BURIED ALIVE. FIVE years OLD. Too YOUNG to UNDERSTAND. Too SMALL to FIGHT BACK. Too INNOCENT to name IT.

That is what molestation feels like: being lowered into the ground while you are still breathing. The dirt of shame covers your voice. Fear packs it tightly around your chest, and you want to scream, but the world above you moves on as if nothing happened. At that age, I did not have words to describe what was taking place. I did not know what the violation meant. I did not understand that this was a breach of my personal space. I did not know it was an infraction on my body. I only knew something inside me broke, and from then, I carried a weight I could not explain, like I was suffocating—buried alive. What came next was learning to survive, hiding behind smiles that came from my lips and not from my eyes. Confused and lonely, I wondered if God remembered that I was down there, in the dark, under the weight of betrayal, pondering if I would ever truly bounce back. What I did not know then was that while I felt buried, God had already marked me as planted.

As the years passed, I carried and buried the pain into everything, including the way I began to see myself: broken and beyond repair. I built walls of protection, which in turn shut out my healing, and I did not realise that the dirt I despised was the very place God wanted to begin my growth. Little by little, God began breaking through the silence—prayer, worship, tears, and therapy—which became the rain that softened the soil around me. After this, I started to believe that what happened to me did not define what God could do through me.

Healing did not happen overnight, as some days I still felt the dirt on my skin as I was plagued by the memories, the triggers, and the pain, but with every breath I took, I learned to begin calling it what it was: not a grave but a garden. Once I came to this realisation, I was able to release the hold on my soul. I got my voice back, learning to speak, bringing light to what once lived in the dark, knowing that after being buried alive, resurrection is possible.

In all this, I learned that to grow daily, we first have to live beneath the surface. When we hide in the shadow of God, He protects us from adversity, works on our hearts, and gives us the wisdom and strength to fight and rise above the issues we face. When He renews our hearts and minds beneath the surface, He grants us the power to conquer all things at the surface level. The 'water' that has been welling up in our hearts from all the hurt we feel will rise from beneath the ground and saturate the surface. In this moment, what is meant to be fruitful will be watered, and what is meant to harm you will be destroyed.

Genesis 2:6 states, *"But there went up a mist from the earth, and watered the whole face of the ground." (KJV).* Now I can look back and see that the soil that once suffocated me became my place of strength, and the parts of me that were broken made me resilient and became my passion and calling. Now, every time I tell my story, I am not just reliving the pain—I am reclaiming my voice—showing others who feel they have been buried alive that dirt is not the end; it is where new life begins.

What was most challenging for me, and what I believe can be most challenging for anyone who encounters this trauma, is the need to move forward with life without dealing with what you experienced. Instead of meeting ourselves where we are, extending ourselves grace like we would another human being, asking for the support we need to move forward, we decorate our soil with new jobs and new relationships. Still, if the roots are choked and tangled with fear, anxiety, anger, and shame, if we do experience growth, our fruits will only reflect what lies beneath the surface. A strong start only begins when we have cultivated the courage to go underground to uproot what does not belong and plant what gives life.

Considering the experience of making a significant life decision, we may spend weeks or months assessing the benefits and drawbacks of making that decision and, even if we do not take a long time to make the decision, the molding of that decision in becoming what we intend for it to be takes time. Yet, even after thorough consideration, a nagging doubt or a persistent feeling may linger. This feeling, often inexplicable and difficult to articulate, may represent the Lord's subtle guidance. It's a silent voice reminding us to reconsider, to pause, or to perhaps choose a different path. But, in these instances, do not be consumed with moving forward, as a weak foundation will only affect who you are truly meant to be. Instead, give God permission to uproot the thorns that are among your flesh.

BYE BYE, *Fear.* Hello **CONFIDENCE.**

For me, fear definitely needs to be the first weed to GO. Fear affects our ability to yearn and long for change, leaving us to wallow in our circumstances. Often, it creeps in quietly and begins to take root by wrapping itself around our dreams, aspirations, and desires to break free, until we forget what hope feels like, having been convinced that hiding is safer than healing. There comes a turning point when you acknowledge that God never designed you to be buried forever, and He is calling you to come up from out of your grave. This is where you choose to say goodbye to fear, not because it is easy, but because you deserve peace.

Saying goodbye does not mean pretending you were never afraid; it means acknowledging the fear that kept you alive and then releasing it so you can begin to thrive. Remember, your state of mind can significantly impact how you move from this level and step into your calling.

How do you choose to see yourself?

Small? Big?
Weak? Strong?
Timid? Bold?

Always remember that **"...God hath not given [you] the spirit of fear; but of power, and of love, and of a sound mind." (2 Timothy 1:7 - KJV).** Going from being fearful to feeling confident is literally a breath of fresh air. Confidence begins to grow in small, intimate moments when you choose to listen to and act according to God's will, despite feeling fear. This is compounded by the first time you use your voice again, the first time you walk into a space that once made your heart race, and the first time you look into the mirror and say, "I am still here by the Grace of God." Each of these choices then becomes an act of rebellion against what hurt you. When you remove fear, you make room for boldness—not arrogance but the quiet confidence that comes from knowing who you are in God.

BYE BYE, *Anxiety*. Hello **PEACE.**

Anxiety follows close behind fear. Who wants to listen to the constant hum of "what ifs" and "not enoughs?" When we calm anxiety, we welcome peace—a stillness that settles the mind and reminds us that we are safe in His hands.

Anxiety is the thief of the joy and peace that the Lord has promised you. It exists to rob you of your desire to lean on and trust the promises of God. You are encouraged to totally surrender your desires to Him and trust His promises to make your life anew. Once you are able to subject your anxiety under the blood of Jesus, you will be able to experience His peace, joy, hope, and love.

We are reminded in His Word, **"Do not be anxious about anything, but in every situation, by prayer and petition, with thanksgiving, present your requests to God. And the peace of God, which transcends all understanding, will guard your hearts and your minds in Christ Jesus." (Philippians 4:6-7 - NIV).** So, if I could ask God for anything in my life, anything that I am bound to receive, I would ask for Peace.

Many of us are victims of the ideologies of the world—the idea to fit in; the idea to look a certain way; the idea to think, act, and be a certain way. The society we live in will, more often than not, shape who we become. Most of the time, we are stuck in our heads, wondering how to do this or that, not being at peace with the magnitude of the blessing we're already dwelling in. The foundation of peace starts with asking God for it. So, the next time you feel like your whole world is crashing down, choose to ask God for PEACE, because peace will help you to be still when all the world around you is shaking. It will help you to experience the presence of God and guide you in living your truth and walking in my purpose.

BYE BYE, *Anger*. Hello **JOY**.

Then comes anger, often born from the places we were hurt but never healed. When we release anger, we invite joy—the ability to enjoy life again, to laugh, to rest, to find beauty, even in ordinary moments. Many of us live in masks daily. We dream of 'the life' we see on social media, which may not even be real. We crave it. We desire to be like the influencers. And it makes us feel defeated when we are not living in other people's truth or lies, and it even troubles our minds because we are not at peace with our lives or with where God has us dwelling at that moment in time. You are invited to say goodbye to anger, so that you can begin to experience joy in His presence as stated in Psalm 16:11 **"Thou wilt shew me the path of life: In thy presence is fulness of joy; At thy right hand there are pleasures for evermore." (KJV).**

Living from a place of joy is not easy. To do so, we will need a complete renewal of thinking. This means we will need to change our values, beliefs, ideas, perceptions, mindsets, and attitudes. Living from this state of being begins in the mind with what we choose to think, believe, and embed in our value system. One thing that we certainly have control over is refocusing our minds. If you think about the news daily, you will certainly not be at peace and may even find it hard to enjoy the simple things in your day-to-day life. But if you choose to acknowledge what takes place in the world, ask God to intervene in those circumstances, and then wilfully free your minds of it, you can celebrate life. We are reminded of His words in Philippians 4:8: **"Finally, brethren, whatsoever things are true, whatsoever things** are honest, whatsoever things are just, whatsoever things are pure, whatsoever things are lovely, whatsoever things are of good report; if there be any virtue, and if there be any praise, think on these things." (KJV).

BYE BYE, *Shame*. Hello **GRACE**.

Shame buries itself the deepest. It convinces us that we are the mistake rather than someone who simply experienced trauma. I had reached a point in life where moving forward required me to go back to my roots. I had written poems as a little girl, and somewhere in all that writing, I lost my voice. Recently, I went back to my primary school and noticed that one of the poems I had written was still hanging on the wall, over two decades later. To start writing again, I had to acknowledge what had caused me to stop in the first place. I thought of it like a ship. Different vessels require different knowledge and techniques to steer. I finally acknowledged that I needed to cause some obstruction in the devil's kingdom to break the waves and start writing again.

What hardships are you facing that are causing you to feel like you are a victim?

You have possibly tried every technique to get out of the situation you are in. But getting out of the situation does not mean you learned the lesson for why you were in that situation. Sometimes we have to be still and allow God to do His work in our lives. When the Father commands you to stop moving in the midst of a struggle, what feels like doing nothing or silently sitting in a peaceful place actually confuses the enemy and serves as a reminder of his defeat. Because God has triumphed and won the victor's crown for us, we fight from a position of victory rather than fight for victory, as evidenced in His Word, **"for everyone born of God overcomes the world. This is the victory that has overcome the world, even our faith."** (1 John 5:4 - NIV). In writing this passage, it became evident that God had so much to say through me that the devil crippled my voice because he saw the destiny for my life. I realised that I no longer have to wrestle with or think about everything. I simply needed to take action because God reminded me that faith without works is dead. What led me to write again was perseverance and finally understanding that what God wants me to say will benefit those for whom it is meant, and then it became simple, knowing **"that the testing of [my] faith produce perseverance and I lack nothing."** (James 1:3-4 - NIV).

Working through healing after trauma can feel like walking barefoot over broken ground. It is painful, slow, and at times, disorienting. But each new seed we plant takes time to grow; every tear you shed waters a new seed; every honest conversation loosens the soil for something new to grow; and every step forward builds resilience. In this process, we should continue to be attentive to His voice by creating a space for introspection and contemplative prayer, by journaling, focusing on a specific passage of scripture, and patiently waiting to hear His voice. Tapping into this gift enriches our spiritual journey, brings us closer to Him, and leads us toward a life filled with purpose, meaning, and fulfillment.

Hearing God's voice often manifests as a sudden clarity, a feeling of knowing something without understanding how we know it. This may be accompanied by a sense of peace or certainty, a feeling of deep resonance with a particular choice or course of action. At other times, His guidance conveys a strong sense of unease or discomfort, a warning signal that prompts us to avoid a particular situation or decision. Uprooting is messy, lacking neatness and order. The soil is stirred up, the ground feels unstable, and that is when we are LOOSED, and here comes the beginning of a new journey, after the weeds are gone, when your new life has room to grow.

You may not have everything figured out, but this is where you choose to begin again and build stronger by being deliberate about what you allow to take root in your heart. Now, you can water your soul with prayer, nurture yourself through patience, and protect the space you are in with boundaries. Over time, roots of truth and strength begin to form beneath the surface, reminding you that God does not waste pain. What once buried you becomes the soil that nurtures and transforms you; your deepest hurt can become the roots of your greatest strength. So dig deep, plant well, and trust the process. The new growth may start small, but what God grows in hidden places will one day stand tall for all to see. Here is a prayer that can remind you of God's goodness and grace as you gain closure in this chapter of your life:

King of the earth, we adore You for all Your handiwork. We exalt You as the Father who spoke and it was done and commanded and it stood fast. Thank You for giving us a spirit not of fear but of power, love, and a sound mind. We adore Your matchless name. We honour and magnify You because You are the mind regulator. Thank You for Your peace that passeth all understanding. Thank You for being our comforter, though in many ways we do not always take comfort in Your Word or live in our truth of having dominion over fear, anxiety, anger, and shame. We confess that in many ways, we have been troubled with inner turmoil and temporarily lose sight of the promises in Your Word. Please forgive us for our thoughts that have strayed. Forgive us for choosing to battle with what You have overcome on our behalf. Despite all the things we have done to step outside of Your perfect will for our lives, we are grateful that You have shown us how to overcome our fears, anxiety, anger, and shame. We acknowledge that You have been carrying us, even when we thought we were alone with our thoughts and feelings. Thank You for Your revelation that has allowed us to see how the devil tried to cripple our minds, and thank You for showing us how we can subdue what tries to steal our peace, joy, confidence, and grace in You. God, even as we give you thanks for all the works You have done in us, we intercede for threefold blessings for the renewal of our minds. For a change in our being. For strength, and for courage to fight against the thoughts in our minds that want us to feel like we are inadequate or that we are lacking anything. Help us to always remember that You are never slack concerning Your promises and Your Word is true. As You do not take joy in Your creation's suffering, help us not to take joy in fear, anxiety, anger, or shame. Please grant us peace of mind and calm our troubled hearts. Continue to open our hearts and minds to Your truth. In Jesus name. Amen.

SELF-DISCOVERY. RENEWED PERSONAL FREEDOM.

"But ye are a chosen generation, a royal priesthood, an holy nation, a peculiar people; that ye should shew forth the praises of him who hath called you out of darkness into his marvellous light:"

—1 Peter 2:9 KJV

CHAPTER 4

PRUNING: LETTING GO OF WHAT NO LONGER SERVES YOU

Now that you have spent some time uprooting seeds that can harm your growth—fear, anxiety, anger, and shame—and have planted new seeds—confidence, peace, joy, and grace—you can enter into the chapter of growth and cultivation. This particular space you will be in will feel different from the previous one. You may experience a bit of emptiness, like an open wound that needs dressing, or you may be trying to understand how you should operate and function in your new norm. Feeling this way is expected as you transition from one point to the next. At this phase of my journey, I learned that good gardens still need pruning.

Growth does not just happen by planting new seeds but also by pruning—a process by which you let go of what no longer serves your growth. In this season, you focus on gently cutting away old patterns, beliefs, habits, and relationships that block the sunlight that is trying to reach what you are nurturing. Your healing is not only directly linked to what you put in but also what you learn to release. The process of pruning can be seen as an ode to nature, where there is continuous shedding, growth, and renewal. It sounds fun, but let me warn you: it will likely be the hardest part of your journey, because you must return to the wound and tend it to support its healing.

Sometimes it feels easier to carry trauma than to turn around and face it. The pain has a way of becoming part of you. When you have been harmed at such a young age, when your body and spirit were assaulted before you ever had the words to scream "this is not right," it gets comfortable and becomes something you learn to cope with. Sitting with childhood trauma, allowing it to seep into your relationships, decisions, and sense of security, can also feel simpler than digging into it. You may think, "this is just who I am" as you grow up. But the persistent anxiety, tightness in your chest when someone stands too close, the way you shrink yourself, the way you like to control everything around you just to feel steady, are undiluted survival instincts dressed up as confidence. Facing that difficult situation meant slowing down and acknowledging what was in front of me, even when life taught me to keep pushing through every emotion I felt.

The process of letting go of what no longer serves me first meant giving a name to something that stole too much from me too early. It meant allowing myself to feel emotions that I had swallowed because I wanted to be strong and unbothered, not human. Call me an armour-bearer if you will, because I had my armour, and that helped me get through everything, though it hindered my growth. In order to move forward, God's word encourages us to **"Remember ye not the former things, neither consider the things of old. Behold, I will do a new thing; now it shall spring forth; shall ye not know it? I will even make a way in the wilderness, and rivers in the desert." (Isaiah 43:18-19 - KJV).** I tell you this to raise your awareness that you need to face it and name it in order to move forward.

In this next season, I want you to focus on pruning by letting go of what can hinder you progressing to the next phase of your journey. I consider this one of the most powerful steps you will take to move toward spiritual development, as you try to silence your inner noise and become steadfast in listening to God's voice at each leg of your journey. It is important to know and understand what you should actually be letting go of. This is where discernment comes in—the capacity to sense what aligns with your deeper truth. It is a spiritual art that helps you acknowledge and understand who or what is placed in your life for a season, and when its time has expired. Discernment does not demand immediate action; it first invites clarity, and clarity gives you the courage to release. At this juncture, you should give yourself permission to evaluate behaviours that have been prevalent in your life but that now only keep you small, as they can continue to hinder your growth. You give yourself permission to acknowledge and set aside those relationships that once felt like shelters but are only keeping you in the shadows. You give yourself permission to acknowledge and renounce beliefs born of survival, knowing that the next phase of your destiny requires a new mindset. What is key to note here is that letting go of what no longer serves you means stepping away from what feels familiar and giving yourself an opportunity to cultivate a new path, with new attitudes and new belief systems, by stepping into the unknown.

Wondering where to start? You can look within. Here are some questions you can ask yourself to determine your starting point.

- What thoughts drain me?
- What habits keep me tied to the same emotion?
- What stories of my life have I repeated countless times that feel like my current truth, even though they are echoes of old wounds?
- What relationships pull me back into versions of myself that I have outgrown?
- What external stimuli cause me to feel and relive past trauma?

Once you have answered these questions, it is time for grief. This is where you embrace your emotions, one last time, while acknowledging that it is time to say goodbye to them. Letting go means acknowledging that this part of your journey is ending, and that there is expectancy—a quietness of imagining that something new will grow in the open space that you have created.

Pruning requires patience, care, and purpose. Just as addressing suffering can feel stark, sometimes cutting off an old branch reveals new vulnerability. However, it also makes it possible for fresh growth to spring up. In the uprooting process, you unearthed the emotions that had taken root and were hindering your journey. Did you dispose of those weeds? If not, now is the time to do so. With each item you let go of, you create room for something more powerful: security, self-assurance, boundaries, happiness, connection, and a sense of value, which is independent of other people's actions. A trimmed plant becomes more authentic to itself, stronger, and more resilient. Its energy is being diverted into new leaves, blossoms, and branches, rather than seeping into old barks. In the same way, your new energy will be focused on nourishing your new growth rather than nursing wounds of the past.

Being transparent, I cannot ignore my own shortcomings, which became evident during my pruning season. Looking back at the situation, I can truly say I was not patient enough with myself, nor did I have an understanding of what healing should look like for me. I wanted to heal, I wanted to confront, and I wanted to move forward, but over time, what I continued to experience taught me that I neither had a clear idea of what being healed and moving forward looked like nor had I totally surrendered my past. After acknowledging this, I was able to vocalise and visualise what healing should look like for me and began working towards that.

One of the first things was to acknowledge that trying to bury the memory does not make it go away. Healing from sexual abuse is not about forgetting what happened or pretending the past did not shape who I am today. In fact, what I experienced was directly linked to how I perceived every relationship, both intimate and platonic. There was always a key to unlock my true feelings. Still, I never really gave that key to anyone, except my husband, because I wanted the power to not care about anyone else's opinion of me. I knew that if I allowed them to get close, it would change my ability to manage how I feel and to understand my responses to their actions. Now there I was at a crossroads, trying to decide whether I wanted to feel free or safe. Holding on to the emotional responses to trauma made me feel safe, but as time progressed, and seeing that they moved on, I felt the need to feel free again, and that is where I acknowledged that letting go allows me to reclaim the trajectory of my own growth. In the same way, when you let go of your past, or even current experiences or challenges that are keeping you in bondage, you are choosing the aspects of yourself that deserve to continue growing.

Pruning is not a kind of punishment for the plant. It is a strategy a gardener will use to remove from it branches that are no longer beneficial to its health, such as growth that previously aided its survival but now prevents it from thriving, twisted stems that obstruct light, or dead wood that weighs it down. The scripture gives us reassurance that pruning is an act of kindness, as seen in John 15:1-3, **"I am the true vine, and my Father is the husbandman. Every branch in me that beareth not fruit he taketh away: and every branch that beareth fruit, he purgeth it, that it may bring forth more fruit. Now ye are clean through the word which I have spoken unto you." (KJV).** The scripture indicates that this process is not seen as removal but rather an act of care. In a similar way, healing encourages you to gradually remove things that no longer contribute to your wellbeing, such as habits that you had developed in the dark times that no longer belong in your life, shame that was never yours to cling to, beliefs you swallowed to survive, and silence that once shielded you but now limits your voice. This analogy takes me back to high school, when all the prospective science majors and agriculturalists would engage in the process of budding and grafting plants. Sometimes you add layers to help a plant thrive, but in the pruning phase, you remove what is preventing it from thriving. In the same way, spiritual discernment invites us to become gardeners of our inner life, not through our own will but through His will, as we are called. God is calling you to remove the trauma that was grafted onto you in order to reveal the elements of who you are. Hereafter, you can begin developing strategies to help you steer onto a new path.

Here are scriptures which can be used as your daily reminder that you are a made new in Christ:

"Therefore, if any man be in Christ, he is a new creature: old things are passed away; behold, all things are become new." (2 Corinthians 5:17 – KJV).

"Trust in the LORD with all thine heart; and lean not unto thine own understanding. In all thy ways acknowledge him, and he shall direct thy paths." (Proverbs 3:5-6 - KJV).

"If a man therefore purge himself from these, he shall be a vessel unto honour, sanctified, and meet for the master's use, and prepared unto every good work." (2 Timothy 2:21 – KJV).

"And not only so, but we glory in tribulations also: knowing that tribulation worketh patience; and patience, experience; and experience, hope: and hope maketh not ashamed; because the love of God is shed abroad in our hearts by the Holy Ghost which is given unto us. For when we were yet without strength, in due time Christ died for the ungodly." (Romans 5:3-6 - KJV).

GROUNDED.

"Therefore, my dear brothers and sisters, stand firm. Let nothing move you. Always give yourselves fully to the work of the Lord, because you know that your labor in the Lord is not in vain."

— -1 Corinthians 15:58 NIV

CHAPTER 5

NURTURING GROWTH: CULTIVATING PATIENCE AND PERSISTENCE

There comes a time when the noise within quiets, not because everything is fine but because the stronghold has lost its power. It is the moment after you tried to hide beneath everything, when all has now been unearthed, and you start listening for your next move. This is the point where your spirit feels weak and brittle, like when the stems of an orchid have yellowed, and you feel like there is no way to prevent it from dying. Very often, we perceive ourselves in this manner after we have silenced the noise of fear, anxiety, anger, and shame.

It is important to remember that growth does not start with perfection but with presence, meaning you are simply being in the moment, ready to utilise the tools that are available. If you have ever cared for an orchid, you know the truth, that what looks dead is often only resting. Beneath the surface of the soil, the roots are still alive and capable of new growth, provided they are nurtured. I am almost sure there is a bright smile on your face when you receive a new orchid that is fresh and blooming. But have you ever nursed a dying orchid back to life? That is one of the hardest tasks possible, and sometimes you may fail. The garden you imagined would flourish because of the hard work you put into it does not always do so. Sometimes, there is one orchid that refuses to smile at you, even after you have nurtured and cared for it over and over again. It literally appears as if it needs nutrients you cannot purchase at a farm store.

When I started writing this as a short devotional, I had no clue why I chose to compare nurturing a dying orchid back to life with speaking life into our difficult circumstances. In fact, I do not usually gush over plants, let alone orchids. My first encounter with orchids was when my husband demanded that an orchid garden be erected at our home. I was all for it because I wanted the space to look beautiful. I figure having a bunch of different colours would translate to beauty once they all bloom. Little did I know, I was about to embark on the most difficult journey that life had to offer. This was not a simple task. Though we hired a gardener to create the garden and plant the orchids, we did not know that the real work would come after that. Just imagine, planting plants meant for cool climates in an extremely hot temperate zone. We had to water the plants daily, once in the morning and once in the afternoon. Not long after that came what I eventually called the inevitable. You miss one or two days of watering the plants, and then they start wilting. I automatically thought, *"Hey, these plants are just not the best for our climate."* They required WAY TOO MUCH WORK. So, I thought, *"Hmmmm, maybe we should get some plants that would perform better in this climate,"* highlighting my lack of patience and determination. My general thought was, *"It would not appear as if I were failing at taking care of the orchids, if I simply got plants that were easier to take care of."* Nonetheless, my husband was very determined to nurture the plants and ensure they survived. He visited the farm store and gathered all the fertilisers and tools he could find to groom the plants.

Because of the form of the root tubers in some species of the genus Orchis, the word "orchid" is derived from the Greek word, *orchis*, meaning *testicle*. The majority of these perennial non-woody plants are terrestrial or epiphytic herbs. This means they grow on other plants rather than those that are rooted in soil. Historically, orchids are rare. Orchids were quite scarce in the Victorian era. It was necessary to transport orchids from the tropics; a process that might have taken months. The only people who could typically afford and appreciate these flowers were those in higher social classes. At that time, orchids were seen as symbols of wealth, luxury, and refined taste.[1] Now imagine

---

[1] Everyday Orchids. (n.d.). Symbolism and meaning of orchids. Everyday Orchids. Retrieved November 22, 2025, from https://everydayorchids.com/find-out-what-orchid-flowers-symbolize-and-mean-2108r/

receiving an orchid as a gift. Even in today's society, it is seen as a luxury. So imagine back then, when the orchids had to transcend borders to land in the hands of their owners. I can only imagine the process undertaken to prepare orchids for transportation to their prospective owners: pruning and trimming parts of the plant that would no longer allow them to grow. In the same way, you will have your pruning season where God allows you to walk through a process, not out of punishment but out of love for your soul, to make room for new growth, where you are able to release the emotions that held you bound, since they cannot be part of the soil which you are expected to thrive in.

Without a doubt, you would have learned much from holding onto and wrestling with these strongholds, but in your pruning season, you understand the lessons you were learning from these moments of fear, anxiety, anger, and shame, and you begin to cut away their hold on your life. This is one of the greatest acts of trust you will ever engage in as you begin to trust God to plant and nurture new seeds in your life.

After all the tools and fertilisers were gathered for the orchid care, the process of bringing them back to life began. For the first couple of days, I was dedicated to nurturing the plants, but as time went on, I just became a mouthpiece, encouraging my husband to water and care for them the best he could. I had once again given up and had no hope that they would survive. One of the key things he did was place a net over the plants, creating the most suitable environment:

indirect sunlight and warmth without burning the plants. This sheltered them from the sun, gave them enough time to absorb the fertiliser sprayed on them, and created a humid environment. This simple principle taught me that in the process of growth, I did not need to expose myself to everything at once, and further taught me to simply create the right environment that nourishes without overwhelming me, and that healing is not a race toward brighter days but developing simple habits to cultivate a more meaningful life.

After about six months of looking wilted and droopy, the orchids began flourishing. Can you imagine, I was most happy to see them thriving: me, the person who had given up on nurturing and bringing them back to life.

Once you reach this stage of the process, when the orchids are no longer droopy, there is not much more you can do except wait. You continue to water, and you trust that the roots begin to spread, absorb nutrients for the plant, and provide what it needs to continue developing, though you cannot see it with your naked eyes. Here you are in a season where you are forced to learn patience, in the form of sacred trust, becoming confident that the process will simply run its course, remembering **"... that all things work together for good to them that love God, to them who are called according to his purpose." (Romans 8:28 – KJV).**

Trusting that God is doing a work for you, you begin to resist the urge to dig into the soil to check on what is taking place, and now you learn that growth can happen in silence. At this point, all you can do is become persistent; that is what growth is: a simple decision to continue showing up for yourself. You must continue the regimen you have developed for your season, simply trusting that what you are doing is working and that you will see the results in due time.

In your own life, patience looks like your dedication to show up for your healing, for your peace, even when you are uncertain of whether the strategies you have employed are working. This may be considered one of the hardest parts of the journey when you have to steady your faith and confidence in the Lord, trusting that the seeds you have planted are developing into roots that are taking hold beneath the surface. This process looks like feeding your mind with what sustains it, by speaking words of life, *"I am bold. I am blessed. I am loved,"* and feeding your body with what honours it—rest, mindfulness, and movement—and feeding your spirit with what centers it: prayer, reflection, and connection.

There we were, four years later, casually driving in from work, when we saw a glimmer of hope: one of six orchids began to bloom. At this time, we realised that no effort was wasted, neither the silence, nor the pruning, nor the waiting. Each phase has its purpose, and what can I say? It is amazing that God, who breathes life into our dying situations, does not give up on us, even when we feel like giving up on ourselves.

Your orchid is a gift that you have to nurture and breathe life into, in order to walk into your destiny. In simple terms, your spirit needed time to remember how to bloom, and now you are resilient, patient, and persistent. I am almost sure you are not expecting an orchid from me, hopefully. Of course, when we speak about gifts, you may think of the birthday gift, the Christmas gift, or the surprise gift we got from our spouse or friend. But, if you are thinking of the spiritual gifts that Paul encourages us to pray for eagerly in 1st Corinthians 12:4-11, you've got the revelation:

"There are different kinds of spiritual gifts, but the same Spirit is the source of them all. There are different kinds of service, but we serve the same Lord. God works in different ways, but it is the same God who does the work in all of us. A spiritual gift is given to each of us so we can help each other. To one person the Spirit gives the ability to give wise advice; to another the same Spirit gives a message of special knowledge. The same Spirit gives great faith to another, and to someone else the one Spirit gives the gift of healing. He gives one person the power to perform miracles, and another the ability to prophesy. He gives someone else the ability to discern whether a message is from the Spirit of God or from another spirit. Still another person is given the ability to speak in unknown languages, while another is given the ability to interpret what is being said. It is the one and only Spirit who

distributes all these gifts. He alone decides which gift each person should have." (NLT).

Never give up on finding your spiritual identity. What if your gift is just your little orchid that needs to be nursed back to life? What if your gift will be realised through prayer, fasting, and supplication? How often do you pray and earnestly seek God's direction for your life? If you knew that the orchid you are nursing back to life is your ultimate journey to tap into your spiritual gifts, how often would you actually pray and earnestly seek His favour?

Christianity can easily become repetitive and even become a chore. Yes, we pray, worship, praise, and read our Bibles as an act of surrender to God. But when we say we surrender, have we truly given our hearts, minds, bodies, and souls to Him? If yes, then we will have renewed thinking.

Sometimes we are led to believe that the only way of life is what we see as the daily standard, the precedent for how we should act and operate. This is not true for orchids. Each one requires its own unique strategy for survival. Your orchids may be your career, finances, relationships, or your desire to unlock your spiritual gifts. Hand in hand you can walk in God's strength, on His path, in His glory, so that He can teach you His strategy to speak life into every dying situation in your life.

You will witness the newness of life through the power God has invested in you. Renewed thinking transforms your mindset and allows you to walk in God's likeness and image. Renewed thinking allows you to identify God-given strategies to help you become grounded in your spiritual talents, cultivate newness in your life, and live in peace. God calls us to change through His Word, **"And be not conformed to this world: but be ye transformed by the renewing of your mind, that ye may prove what is that good, and acceptable, and perfect, will of God." (Romans 12:2 - KJV).**

HEALED.

"For I know the plans I have for you," declares the Lord, "plans to prosper you and not to harm you, plans to give you hope and a future."

—Jeremiah 29:11 - NIV

CHAPTER 6

BUDDING POSSIBILITIES: LIVING A LIFE OF PURPOSE AND MEANING

L iving from a place of healing feels distinctively different when you have truly done the work that allows you to feel whole, even in your brokenness. This leg of the journey taught me that growth has quiet seasons. Think about the moments where hope and patience feel like the only two phenomena holding things together when growth and progress are invisible. You have played your part by uprooting and planting the seeds needed for this stage. You have let go of what no longer serves you, so all you can do is sit patiently, be persistent, and not become weary in the process, holding onto God's promise, knowing that growth is sometimes slow and quiet, happening beneath the surface and then, before you know it, there is a shift and you can now see what has been developing.

Just as buds form on branches long before they bloom, small signs of change begin to emerge in a life rooted in healing. They might look like gentle sparks of curiosity, new desires, moments of unexpected courage, or the soft pull toward something greater. These are my budding possibilities—the early whispers of purpose and meaning, revealing themselves and asking for my attention. The Bible says, **"See, I am doing a new thing! Now it springs up; do you not perceive it? I am making a way in the wilderness and streams in the wasteland." (Isaiah 43:19 – NIV).** These budding desires, dreams, and stirrings within you are God's whispers of renewal—proof that you are not only being restored, but prepared for purpose. In this phase, you will step into a space to live a purposeful and meaningful life by identifying and utilizing your spiritual gifts.

The gifts which God gives us are not merely personal strengths but rather are divinely ordained tools for building the kingdom and extending God's love to the world. These unique talents and abilities allow us to contribute positively to His kingdom and to the greater good of society by spreading the gospel and ministering to people in our everyday lives. This chapter of my life, in which I was tasked with examining my purpose, taught me that it is crucial to recognise and embrace these gifts to experience a profound sense of purpose and fulfillment in my spiritual journey.

At this juncture, there is also a realisation of the importance of abiding in God's presence. Just as Jesus teaches in John

15:5, the vine and branches grow simply by remaining connected: **"I am the vine; you are the branches. If you remain in me and I in you, you will bear much fruit; apart from me you can do nothing." (NIV).** Your purpose grows naturally when you stay rooted in Him—when you choose truth, healing, and alignment with who He says you are.

The process of identifying spiritual gifts begins with introspection and prayer. Since you have cultivated patience and persistence, you are now at the point of spiritual listening, where you begin to discern and listen for God's voice by engaging in quiet reflection and asking God to reveal the unique talents and abilities He has placed in you. You can ask yourself questions like:

- *What inspires me daily?*
- *What task am I excited to do without external pressure?*

Answering these questions will also allow you to seek an answer from God on which aspect of your purpose aligns with what we consider natural passions, and to receive divine guidance on how to begin unlocking these talents and start impacting lives. During this process, it is important to avoid comparing yourself to others and to recognise that your gifts are unique and tailored to God's plan.

In the spirit of sowing, remember that different sowers can sow different seeds. Even if the same seeds are sown by two different individuals, the results will be different, once the process is not the same. Even if the process is replicated, the difference in the soil can still yield a different result. Bearing this in mind, each individual contributes to the whole in a unique and essential way. There is no single model of spiritual giftedness.

Prayer is another component of this process. It is indispensable, as it is necessary to employ this measure to develop awareness of, understand, and utilise your spiritual talents. When we employ a prayerful posture in all that we do, we open ourselves to hearing God's voice, allowing Him to reveal insights we would have otherwise missed if we were not being guided by the Holy Spirit.

In moments of being prayerful, you can choose a scripture to focus on. In this case, you can meditate on 1 Peter 4:9-11, **"Offer hospitality to one another without grumbling. Each of you should use whatever gift you have received to serve others, as faithful stewards of God's grace in its various forms. If anyone speaks, they should do so as one who speaks the very words of God. If anyone serves, they should do so with the strength God provides, so that in all things God may be praised through Jesus Christ. To him be the glory and the power for ever and ever. Amen." (NIV)**. The scripture expresses God's promise that we are all given spiritual gifts and that if we ask anything of Him, He will answer us. Following this, you can ask God to show you your strengths and how you can utilise them in service to Him. These strategies will assist you in this very active process, which requires persistent engagement with God and the patience to listen for His response while quieting both internal and external noise. Here is a prayer you can say to God to ask Him to reveal your gifts to you:

Father, I adore You through my acknowledgement that You are God and King over my life. I celebrate You for Your handiwork and acknowledge You for the gift You have bestowed upon me. I give You glory for the victory I won when You overcame this world. Even as I celebrate the victory You have won for me and this world, I admit that I have fallen short. In many instances, I failed to understand the lessons You are teaching. Because I couldn't see Your work being done, I failed the test many times. Forgive me for being bitter and frustrated each time You tried to teach me something. Forgive me for the times I complained that things were too tough, when You were simply taking me on a path to unearth my spiritual gifts. Forgive me for doubting my place and purpose on this earth. Thank You for opening my eyes to see the work that You are doing in my life. Thank You for giving me the relationships I needed to help me through life each time I thought I had failed. Thank You for giving me the opportunity for a do-over every day. Trust me, I am never taking that for granted. As I try to focus on learning all the lessons that are preparing me to walk into my destiny, I give You thanks for renewing my mind, for helping me subdue my thoughts, and for giving me the strength to take bold steps with the knowledge I have gained from these lessons. Help me to walk in the newness of life. You know my heart and where I lack. You know my destiny. Prepare me for what is ahead, and help me remember that You are the greatest teacher and that You have my back in every situation. As I continue on this journey, I ask that You create space for me to hear from You, to recognise my spiritual talents, and to use them boldly to serve You. In Jesus' name. Amen.

One key thing to remember is that this process requires persistence. You may not hear from God immediately after this prayer, but this creates a posture of expectation and allows you to have one strategy to prepare you to hear His voice. Once you have identified your spiritual gift, you can use it in service to God and others. This will look like active involvement in your church community through participation in relevant ministries, mission work, and evangelism, in the form of even a simple act of kindness or compassion toward others around you, which spreads the gospel and teaches God's love.

In my journey of self-discovery and learning to live from a place of meaning, I discovered that the possibilities are vast and varied; I would only be limited by my imagination and willingness, so I dare to dream. Consider your strengths: are you a gifted communicator, a compassionate listener, a skilled organizer, a creative artist, or a compassionate caregiver? Each of these gifts can be utilized in countless ways to serve God's purpose.

Here is my own experience. I did not initially consider my communication skills to be spiritual gifts, and there I was, searching for my purpose, trying to determine which office in the church I fit into. Initially, I limited my calling to one gift—singing—but soon realized it was not limited to ministering through singing. In a period when I felt like I had lost my voice and was totally ignoring that calling, I found the new additions through prayer and supplication.

For a long time, I perceived my communication skills as a simple area in which I was good. This talent took the form of listening, talking, connecting, explaining, and expressing. During the discovery phase, I noticed people gravitated towards me when they needed someone to talk to. What also became evident is that when I spoke from the heart, it resonated with many people. When I prayed, the prayers God allowed me to share would comfort and open doors for those around me to hear from God. In both circumstances, I began to feel a sense of peace and alignment whenever I used my voice to sing or speak, and realised that it made others feel uplifted and encouraged. This process also did not feel forced, but felt natural and guided by someone bigger than me. As time progressed and I opened myself to the various tenets of communication, I noticed that I was a listening ear to many people who needed to express themselves for a moment to release what they were experiencing, and to encourage others with the stories I had lived through. With these exchanges, over time, I began to discover that my words did not just fill a space; they moved people through clarity, comfort, and direction, and that the space I created for those who wanted to express themselves was sacred. In that moment, I realized this was not just an expertise but a gift—something deeper which I was being called to. After realising this, I learned how to honour this gift by tapping into it.

Learning to utilise this gift required a deeper understanding of what it entails: knowing when to listen and when to speak, including what to speak about. Gradually, there came an understanding of a need to quiet both internal and external noises, a process by which I was required to *Silence Me* to hear His voice as the dominant leading sound, necessary to hear and understand what needed to be said through me. When the nudge came in those moments of silence and reflection, I began to be obedient by ministering to individuals, asking simple questions to prompt their own reflection, or simply sharing a perspective based on the instruction received from God. The next step was to embrace authenticity.

Initially, I was invulnerable. Every nudge that came led to an action, but with little zeal to connect it to personal experiences when illustrating a specific topic. What I noticed was that continuing to unlock this gift led me to face more challenges, which I needed to overcome in order to develop and share the strategies others facing similar challenges needed to utilise. Having now understood the gift which was given to me, the need to be more honest and vulnerable emerged. In the moments of ministering to others, I began to feel open and honest about my story, struggles, and growth. That is the strongest my voice felt, and it became evident that being real is more perfect than being perfect.

What came next was intentionally practicing my communication skills, active listening, and sharing little devotionals as I was led. I accepted that communication is a form of service; whether encouraging someone, explaining something clearly, or bringing calm to a situation, I am serving. Understanding communication as a spiritual gift allowed me to see myself differently, and this shift in perspective changed everything. I began to see myself as someone who does not simply communicate well but carries messages that matter, and this helped me to embrace my voice as a tool.

The key idea is to identify your strengths. Once you do, you will begin to see them as unique talents, and then you will seek opportunities to use them in ways that align with your purpose, values, and passion. Do not be afraid to become experimental during this phase. It is important to note that you will need to step outside your comfort zone, as this may push you to try something new and utilise your gift in unexpected avenues of service. This can mean becoming bold to talk about your circumstances and how you overcame them, even if you were not like that in the past. In doing this, your "why" is gradually introduced as you begin to understand why you have been gifted in the ways you have and how this will help you fulfill your calling. Think of this process like petals slowly opening to the morning sun, where your life begins to make sense in small, holy moments, and you begin to actualise through renewed passion, regained hope, and a brave "yes."

The scripture reminds us that God's plans for our lives are intentional and hopeful, as seen in Jeremiah 29:11, **"For I know the plans I have for you, declares the LORD, plans to prosper you and not to harm you, plans to give you hope and a future." (NIV).** This reminds us of the budding possibilities that occur in our lives, once we have given God our YES. The simple YES affords us a never-ending journey of continuous growth and development, where we embrace our gifts in an ongoing process of self-discovery and service to God's kingdom.

When you begin to bloom into God's purpose, always remember that His guiding hand is what you ought to seek to push you in the right direction. Approach this chapter of your life with humility and discernment, having expectancy, knowing that while **"In their hearts humans plan their course, but the LORD establishes their steps." (Proverbs 16:9 – NIV).**

Leaning on God for direction will allow you to avoid prideful thinking and leaning on your own understanding, as stated in Proverbs 3:5-6, **"Trust in the LORD with all thine heart; And lean not unto thine own understanding.**

In all thy ways acknowledge him, And he shall direct thy paths." (KJV). God's promise to guide you is also seen in Isaiah 30:21, which states, **"and thine ears shall hear a word behind thee, saying, This is the way, walk ye in it, when ye turn to the right hand, and when ye turn to the left." (KJV).**

Humility reminds us that our gifts are not ours but are entrusted to us for a divine purpose, and without it, we risk misusing them for our own gratification. This is where discernment comes in. This simple, yet powerful tool allows us to self-introspect. Are we driven by a desire to serve God and His people, or are we driven by our own motives, working with a desire for recognition? Prayerful reflection and also guidance from God through our mentors can often confirm or question our intended actions. For example, at the time I was writing this book, I came to a point of questioning: *Is this really what I should be speaking about now? Is this the correct title for the book?* But in two separate spiritual instances, one being prayer and the other a conversation, the words shared directly aligned with what God shared as His expectation of me months prior. As such, I felt a new sense of empowerment to proceed along the path, which had become much clearer. It is also key to note that God's purpose for our lives may not be defined by grand achievements, be it a simple act of kindness or love on display—simple expressions of His love toward mankind.

Understanding your spiritual gifts and living from a place of purpose is a transformative journey, where, in one-on-one time with God, you are afforded the opportunity to develop a deeper connection to Him. Embrace the journey with humility, prayer, and a willingness to serve, and in due season, you will understand the role you are called to.

SEVENFOLD ABUNDANCE.
BLESSINGS. NEW BEGINNINGS

"Forget the former things; do not dwell on the past. See, I am doing a new thing! Now it springs up; do you not perceive it? I am making a way in the wilderness and streams in the wasteland."

—Isaiah 43:18-19 - NIV

CHAPTER 7

HARVESTING THE FRUITS OF SPIRITUAL DISCERNMENT

The journey toward spiritual discernment is a transformative process of self-discovery. As we have explored in previous chapters, this process of spiritual development is never ending, and takes us on a path that requires us to be resilient amid adversity, to embrace change, to uproot seeds which hinder our growth and plant seeds which support our growth, to let go of what no longer serves us, to cultivate patience and persistence, and to begin living a life of purpose and meaning in order to harvest the fruits of spiritual discernment.

As we silence our external and internal noise, we cultivate a stillness that allows us to hear God's voice, understand ourselves and our purpose more deeply, and begin to unearth our spiritual identity. When I began writing this book, I believed I would focus on silencing external noise by assessing how society creates a space where we are positioned to focus on external ways of operating, rather than on functioning as God designed us to. But in my own journey, I soon realized that silencing our internal noise is most important, as this, in turn, shapes what we consume from the world. Silencing the noise within you begins with a process of introspection, which requires a willingness to look inward and honestly examine your thoughts, feelings, and behaviors. This should not be seen as a self-critical exercise aimed at finding fault with oneself, but rather a compassionate exploration of your inner landscape, whereby you will be able to understand your shortcomings, address these shortcomings, and create a space for spiritual discernment to begin, allowing you to create a deeper connection with God.

In this process, a focus is placed on gentleness and self-compassion, recognising that our imperfections and vulnerabilities are part of our humanity and are subject to God's love and renewal. Harvesting the fruits of spiritual discernment involves developing and using strategies that help us understand where we are and create a pathway to where we want to be.

One powerful tool for self-reflection is **journaling**. This takes me back to my childhood. When I was a little girl, I generally engaged in journaling. I spoke candidly about what I experienced on a daily basis, the challenges these experiences presented, and the strategies I can use to mitigate them, and gave myself the chance to assess each area with a positive outlook, creating a charge for how I should operate the next day. This was interrupted when my diary was stolen, sparking a chain of events that led me to refrain from writing my inner thoughts to process and to adopt new ways of operating in the wake of that incident.

Years went by, and before making journaling a habit to help me unlock my spiritual fruits, the only time I could think of marrying the process to was immediately after giving birth to my son. After receiving the journal from a friend, I noted that it was challenging me to document the first 90 days after giving birth. I encouraged myself to commit to the process and, each day, wrote in that journal, making special notes about the things I wanted to do that day. The journal also allowed me to document the emotions I was experiencing each day.

In the beginning, I felt crippled, having done a cesarean section, experiencing challenging postnatal moments, and not being able to do most things on my own. Nevertheless, as I continued on this journey, writing down my daily thoughts, feelings, and desires, I noted that a recurring trend was that I wanted the same set of activities each day, and I was leaning on the same set of people. This process of journaling directly documented the struggles I experienced, assisted me in processing them, and helped me identify what I needed to do and what external support I truly needed to help me feel like my best self while navigating what I consider one of the most challenging phases of life's journey. Having made all those notes, I was able to dissect the experiences and identify the values and principles I used to navigate this space. Not only was this useful in the moment, but reflecting on this season also allowed me to create a value-weighting system for my friendships. Following this, I prayed a simple, deliberate, and powerful prayer: *"Lord, some of my friendships have expired. Teach me to accept this. Amen."* His soft, simple answer was, *"Some persons you have held on to for years are not meant to step into your next season with you."* Though this was hard to hear and accept, and while the process was challenging, God stood firm with me throughout the season of shedding, and I never even had to be the one to end any of those friendships.

Through journaling, you can begin to unearth underlying beliefs that shape your perception of yourself and the world. It is a process by which you are able to articulate all that happens within and around you, and question them by asking, *"Are these thoughts and actions in alignment with my deepest spiritual aspiration? Do they create an avenue for me to step into my calling, or are they hindrances to it?"* Once you do this, you can seek divine intervention from God through His guidance on how to respond to these matters.

Another avenue for self-discovery is **mindful observation**. This is a process that involves deep introspection into your present circumstances or experiences without any form of judgment. The absence of judgment allows you to fully understand and be present in the moment without holding yourself accountable for any action taken. You can cultivate this awareness through practices like meditation, paying attention to how your body reacts to stimuli such as: *Do you take a deep breath when you feel in danger, or do you respond with a particular emotion when you smell, see, taste, or touch something? How do you interact with others?* My first interaction with this process was when I began therapy. At this moment, I was asked what my triggers were. This was a question in relation to what affects my day-to-day life, processing the trauma of sexual abuse. The quickest answer I gave was *"I don't know,"* but after reflecting, I recognized that I have a very good understanding of what triggers me. To delve deeper into this process, I was tasked with identifying the triggers I experienced, taking into account all five senses and interpersonal interactions. After writing these down, I was able to determine how I responded to the trigger, what thoughts I had in the moment, and what emotions I experienced. This attentive presence allowed me to observe my emotional responses in real time, recognize patterns of reactivity, and discover triggers that set off specific responses. Doing this allowed me to determine which strategies I needed to utilise to address these issues by cultivating a more nuanced understanding of my emotional landscape and by responding to the circumstances rather than reacting to them.

The regular practice of these methods allowed me to begin discerning a deeper connection between my experiences and my spiritual identity. Having identified recurring themes through my journaling and mindfulness, I was able to understand the direction God was leading me in for ministry.

In the same way, when you engage in these processes, you can begin to notice consistent patterns in your emotions, understand unresolved conflicts, reveal hidden talents, and discover your underlying spiritual gifts. An example of a theme you could identify is compassion. If journaling helps you identify a need to be caring and loving toward others, it may point to a ministry of service or even caregiving. Another example could be your struggle with anger, indicating a deep call to forgiveness, both of yourself and others. The call to forgiveness would allow you to pour into others when they experience hardship with forgiveness, when they have been wronged. Both insights provide valuable clues towards understanding your unique spiritual path.

Having a deeper understanding of oneself is just the beginning of the process. Harvesting the fruits of spiritual discernment is not just an internal process. It is fundamentally intertwined with your relationship with God. As you begin to cultivate a deeper connection with God, you will gain a clearer perspective of yourself and your place in the world. Through prayer, fasting, meditation, and stillness to hear His voice, you open yourself to the transformative power of God's grace, allowing a deeper understanding of your inherent worth and God-given potential. When you do this, you begin to recognize that your spiritual identity is not something you create on your own. It is a gift, a blueprint, revealed through a relationship with the Divine.

Throughout biblical literature, God is presented as the source of spiritual discernment, as evidenced in several passages. In Corinthians, Paul teaches that spiritual truth can only be understood through a relationship with God, mediated by the Holy Spirit. He further examines this fact by highlighting that the natural person neither understands nor accepts ideologies which are of the Spirit of God, as they are unable to spiritually discern them, as seen in the verses: **"Which things also we speak, not in the words which man's wisdom teacheth, but which the Holy Ghost teacheth; comparing spiritual things with spiritual. But the natural man receiveth not the things of the Spirit of God: for they are foolishness unto him: neither can he know them, because they are spiritually discerned." (1 Corinthians 2:13-14 – KJV).**

Another example of God as the source of spiritual discernment is seen in Daniel 2, where Daniel relies on God through prayer for wisdom to interpret Nebuchadnezzar's dream. In response to this prayer, God gave Daniel a dream to unveil the mystery. Daniel's relationship with God is directly juxtaposed with Nebuchadnezzar's relationship with his pagan wise men and his dependence on them. The passage explicitly emphasizes that spiritual discernment comes from God, not from human wisdom.

Harvesting the fruits of spiritual discernment is not always easy. It is directly linked to the process of self-discovery, which must be actualised to move toward spiritual discernment. Spiritual discernment relies on deeper reflection, greater humility, and renewed and constant reliance on God's guidance. Within this process, trusting what we see, hear, and feel is paramount, even when we do not fully understand where our actions are leading us. Instances which appear unclear require deeper faith, which assures us that God is present, guiding and supporting us every step of the way.

To unlock spiritual discernment, one must already understand their spiritual identity, and you can begin exploring different areas of ministry or even finding spiritual mentors that align with your passion. A spiritual mentor can pray with you in difficult moments, seek guidance from God on your behalf, challenge limiting beliefs, and create a space for you to explore vulnerable thoughts and feelings. Spiritual discernment is like tending to a garden. You have tilled the soil of your heart, planted seeds of listening through prayer and fasting, and patiently wait for God to reveal what has been growing beneath the surface. In due season, there comes a harvest.

So what does harvesting the fruits of spiritual discernment truly mean? Simply put, it represents the gathering of blessings, insights, and transformation that mature when we choose to listen deeply and follow God's leading. Here are some fruits that you can expect to reap as you move through this process:

1. **Clarity of Purpose:** Discernment removed the weeds of confusion. When I first began identifying

my purpose, I was still unsure and doubtful. I questioned everything, seeking much clarity on what direction to move into, and wrestled with whether I was truly hearing from God or if the thoughts were simply intrusive. Months after I got the assignment to write this book, I went to the altar, praying and asking God to speak through me, and the simple words came to clarify that what had been revealed months prior and the path I was to embark on were a directive from God. In that moment, there came a great clarity in my purpose. I had all the tools and only needed to act, and in that moment, I finally acknowledged what was mine to carry. Following that final revelation, I made a vow to always obey God, even when I had no clue how the things He instructed me to do would fall into place, impact my life, and, importantly, be a light to others around me. What did I gather in the harvest? Clarity, focus, and a purposeful life rooted in God's will.

2. **Inner Peace:** In managing my experience with trauma, the main goal was to have internal resolution because I had a clear understanding that I cannot make anyone sorry for what they did. Initially, my world and the abuser's world would collide. It was a scenario where I was simply too young to remove myself from the same space. Because of this, my main focus was utilising strategies that would allow me to feel some level of calm and comfort while analysing whether I was physically exposed to the

current threat, or simply staying afloat and not showing my immediate emotions to him. I did not want him to sense the fear I lived in at any given moment when he was in my space. While I used fear to guard against any other such experience, fear was crippling and did not allow me to have the peace that was needed to move forward from the experience. Because peace needed a space to grow, I had to trust God and let go of the fear. *What can you gather in this harvest?* A deep, steady calm; not the absence of a struggle but the presence of God in the midst of it all.

3. **Purified Desires:** I don't think we talk enough about how spiritual growth can create a space for one to gain interest in the things of God and lose interest in the things of the world, which once entertained us. It also forces you to confront behaviours that once felt normal. In this process, we see how spiritual discernment cuts away self-centered motives. It shifts the perspective from what you desire for yourself to what God wants to do through you to edify His name and to lead others to Him. *What did I gather from this harvest?* Freedom from worldly desires and the goodness of Godly desires.

4. **Growth in virtue:** Your new beginning starts with the gradual development of a moral character by becoming consistent in your inclination to do what is right in God's eyes. When you begin to practice good

actions, they become more natural over time. You will discover that you have formed a character, not merely behaviours or habits. What can you gather from this harvest? Patience, courage, wisdom, gratitude, and humility.

5. **Awareness of God's Presence:** Discernment trains the eyes to understand God's blueprint. You will begin to understand when God is speaking to you directly, when He is giving you an instruction to share with someone, or when He is speaking to you through someone else. When I began to develop the gift of discernment, I was able to understand when God was speaking to me in my everyday conversations, in silence, through scripture, and in unexpected moments. *What did I gather from this harvest?* A growing sensitivity to God's voice and friendship.

6. **Confidence in decision-making:** Discernment builds trust. Eventually, you will be able to step forward without doubt or fear, knowing that He is the one who guides you in all you do. *What can you gather from this harvest?* Boldness, resilience, and freedom from decision paralysis.

7. **A Life that Nourishes Others:** A heart shaped by discernment becomes softer and allows room for compassion for others. You begin to see those around you as seedlings in God's garden who need care and

111

are able to meet people where they are in need. Your words then begin to encourage, your actions heal, and your presence brings light. This is when your life is nourishing others. *What can we gather from this harvest?* Empathy, gentleness, the grace to forgive, tangible actions that bless homes, heal communities, and the world.

Spiritual discernment requires you to discover yourself. It is a process of planting, listening by allowing what you plant to take root, cultivating by being obedient, and transformation is the harvest. It is a path of continuous learning and refinement, a constant unfolding of who you are in the light of God's unwavering love.

This journey, even with its challenges, brings with it an unparalleled sense of purpose, belonging, and profound joy. It will transform your life, enriching every aspect of your existence. It is, ultimately, a testament to the transformative power of God.

REFLECTION

EVOLUTION: STILLNESS. DISCERNMENT. SPIRITUAL GROWTH.

The journey of silencing the world around and one's inner thoughts is lifelong, fostered by a continuous need for spiritual enrichment. The preceding chapters have provided tools and frameworks that can be utilised to foster spiritual discernment. The path ahead requires ongoing support, as you must nurture what you have begun cultivating. I charge you to create your roadmap for continued growth by developing your spiritual toolbox and identifying resources to deepen your understanding and strengthen your faith.

One of the most valuable resources for continued spiritual growth is engaging with the Holy Bible. In reading this book, you will be able to learn and study His Word, which will guide how you operate. You can also engage with insightful, biblically sound literature, which can offer a wealth of wisdom and expand your understanding of spiritual principles and practices. Start by exploring diverse authors and perspectives that resonate with you, and focus on books that address your current needs and stage of spiritual development.

Spiritual growth also involves community. Connecting with a supportive community allows you to share your journey, receive encouragement, and learn from others. This can take the form of various church groups, once the environment or space allows for spiritual development. The environment should allow for small group studies, retreats, and workshops designed to foster spiritual growth and connection. Once you join these groups, you should connect with a safe, supportive environment to share experiences, ask questions, and learn from others on a similar journey. The shared experience of faith and spiritual practice can be a source of deep strength and encouragement.

In addition to books and community, mentorship can profoundly affect your spiritual journey. In seeking a mentor, you are charged with identifying someone with significant spiritual longevity who is God-centered and being led by God. You will need discernment to help you identify this person. This individual should be able to provide personalised guidance, support, and accountability along your journey. There should be room for openness and vulnerability, with this mentor serving as a sounding board for your thoughts and feelings, offering wisdom and insight from their own experiences. A mentor's guidance should be supportive and not prescriptive, unless God gives him or her a direct revelation on what you are required to do in a particular season. Finding a mentor can entail contacting people whose lives and knowledge you respect, joining a spiritual community with designated mentors, or looking for spiritual directors within your own faith. Finding someone who connects with you, whom you respect and trust, and whose advice feels genuine and encouraging is crucial. The mentor-mentee connection should be reciprocal, with you contributing to the mentor-mentee dynamic.

Since spiritual growth is a personal and evolving process, you are also encouraged to create space for prayer and fasting. See these activities as those that foster focus on God and help you overcome barriers that affect you hearing from Him. Both present you with an opportunity for spiritual humility and devotion, while eliminating distractions. Both prayer and fasting are evident in the book of Daniel, with Chapter 9:3 specifically highlighting prayer and fasting, and Chapter 10 highlighting the conditions under which Daniel fasted and his response from God. These tools were utilised to understand God's plan and created space for the vision through which Daniel gained spiritual insight.

Here is an outline for prayer which you can utilise:

1. Choose a fixed daily time during which you can avoid distractions.

2. Create an environment for stillness.
3. Ask God to speak.
4. Be silent and wait to hear God speak.
5. Noticing by identifying what thoughts or even scriptures come to mind.

Silence is where listening is trained. This technique can help you build a framework for spiritual listening and discernment.

Here is a strategy for fasting that you can utilise:

1. Look at fasting as making room and not punishing the body.
2. Identify what is currently dimming your alertness and make a decision to give it up.
3. Turn moments of hunger into a simple prayer. *"Lord, I hunger for You. Amen."* This highlights awareness and dependence on God.
4. Set aside time for fasting.
5. Identify focus scriptures.

As spiritual listening and discernment grow, you will identify the fruits of the Spirit. Creating space for prayer and fasting is an act of consent. You are saying, *"God, I am ready to hear You speak."*

You have the chance to learn more about yourself on your journey. Confronting negative aspects of yourself, dealing with challenging emotions, and striving for greater self-awareness are common components of spiritual development. Professional assistance may be necessary for this journey, especially if you're facing serious personal difficulties.

Seeking assistance from a therapist or counsellor is an act of self-care and dedication to your overall well-being, not a show of weakness. Your chosen path should be genuine to you, representing your distinct character, beliefs, and life experiences. This all-encompassing strategy is essential for sustaining a robust, healthy spiritual practice and nourishing your spirit. Remember, spiritual maturity is not measured by perfection but by a commitment to ongoing growth and a deep, persistent desire to connect with God. This journey requires humility, acknowledging that there is always more to learn, more to understand, more to grow into.

Finally, remember the importance of patience and self-compassion. Spiritual growth is a gradual process of planting, weeding, pruning, and reaping. Where there are moments of doubt, setbacks, and challenges, be kind to yourself, acknowledge your imperfections, and celebrate your progress, no matter how small. This journey is about becoming who God has designed you to be and walking in that grace. Embrace the process, trust the journey, and maintain faith in the ultimate goodness and purpose inherent in your spiritual growth. The ultimate reward is not a perfect spiritual life but a life characterised by love, compassion, resilience, and a deeper connection with the Divine. The journey, with all its ups and downs, shapes and forms us, refining our spirit and making us more compassionate, understanding, and empathetic individuals.

PRAYER

Heavenly Father, we thank You for being the peace speaker. We adore You that even as waves crash, You can remain asleep in peace. Lord, how excellent is Your peace that we can dwell in a safe space if we believe. Thank You for always controlling the wind and waves in our lives. While we do not always live in consciousness of Your peace, today we acknowledge You as the peace that passeth all understanding. We complain that we are never at peace, that we do not have what the world has, that we feel left out, that we are tormented, all the while not accepting the peace that You have given us. But, Father, in all we do, help us to acknowledge the presence of Your peace. While we sometimes turn away from the peace You gave us, we thank You that You have renewed our minds and done a new work in us, so that we can desire to live and dwell with You in perfect peace. We thank You that we have had relationships and opportunities that have brought peace to our lives, even when we were not dwelling in Your peace. We thank You that those circumstances were a temporary fix, until we realised the need to dwell fully in Your peace. Father, now we open our hearts to You. Even as You rebuked the wind and sea, we believe that You will rebuke every storm in our lives. We believe that peace will be still in every situation. That we will come to live in peace with our minds and with our thoughts. We declare that we will never have to worry when storm clouds are raging because Your still, small voice will whisper "PEACE BE STILL." Help us to dwell in Your peace, always. In Jesus' name. Amen.

ACKNOWLEDGMENTS

This book is a special one. It required patience, obedience, and transparency so that I could encourage you with authenticity. My village was paramount to the completion of *Silencing Me: Overcoming Obstacles to Spiritual Discernment*, and this work would not have been possible without their support, encouragement, and contributions.

I am deeply grateful to Pastor Jillian Thomas for writing the foreword and for beautifully setting the spiritual and thematic context for this book. Your insight and wisdom laid a powerful foundation for what follows.

My sincere thanks to Tiffany Scafe Norman for her thoughtful endorsement, offering a psychology-based perspective while seamlessly marrying faith and emotional wellness. Your voice adds depth and balance to this work.

I also extend heartfelt appreciation to Tiffany Wright for her faith-based endorsement and for affirming the message and purpose of this book.

To my husband, Chevaughn Miller, thank you for creating the space—emotionally, mentally, and practically—for me to write and to embark on this deeply personal journey. Your love, patience, and unwavering support mean more than words can express.

I am forever grateful to my parents, Jacqueline and Wendell Whyte, and to my siblings, who have taught me discipline, love, respect, and so many values that have shaped the woman I am today. Your prayers and encouraging words sustain me daily.

Special thanks to Daive Richards for his support with Graphic representations that enhanced the visual expression of this project and helped bring its message to life.

Thank you to my editor and publisher, Cleveland McLeish, for guidance, professionalism, and commitment. Your expertise and patience were invaluable throughout this process.

Above all, God, I thank You for speaking to me so that I could speak to others. Thank You for walking me through a process that strengthened my spiritual listening and discernment. It was not easy, but becoming more Christ-like rarely is. One thing is certain—I am committed to growing with You.

ABOUT THE AUTHOR

Samontia Whyte Miller is a dynamic author, speaker and entrepreneur, dedicated to empowering Christians to lead with confidence and purpose. She is the Founder and CEO of Transform You, a movement focused on personal growth and positive change, through guided spiritual support by inspiring many with her personal stories and lessons learned from biblical principles and teachings. This strategy is evident in Transform You: Once Driven, Forever Free, for which she is the Author.

Through her work, Samontia encourages Christians to embrace their voices, own their stories, and step boldly into their potential. Her passion for uplifting others shines through her writing, speaking engagements, and entrepreneurial ventures, making her a powerful force for God's kingdom. Her passion for communication is evident in her professional expertise as she holds a Bachelor of Arts in Integrated Marketing Communications and a Master of

Business Administration in Management Information Systems.